# Festivals

## A letter from the Author

Hello,

**Welcome to Festivals!**

*Festivals are part of our lives. We have personal festivals, like birthdays. And we have big festivals, like Carnival and Christmas and New Year. Then there are national festivals, like Independence Day and Republic Day. In some towns, there are special, local festivals to celebrate local events.*

*There are also the religious festivals: Christmas, Lent and Easter in the Christian World, Ramadan and Eid for Muslims, Diwali for Hindus, Hanukkah for Jews, Buddha's Birthday in Asia... Now there are modern festivals, like Women's Day and World Environment Day, too. The list goes on and on.*

*Many festivals have their own food and celebrations. Some festivals occur in different forms in different countries. And some change their dates, like Valentine's Day (14th February in Europe and North America, June in Brazil).*

*Let's try to understand these differences. In this way, we can find out about people in different places and cultures. Why are they different? Perhaps, through their festivals, we can understand other people better.*

*In 'Festivals', we have information and pictures about festivals in different places. There are also opportunities to reflect, to compare, and to do research. FESTIVAL EYE suggests things that you can find out. There are also some fun projects on festivals. Now, over to you!*

**Susan Holden**

# contents

## TO THE TOPICS USERS

**VOCABULARY** You can find the key vocabulary for every article in the **WORD FILE** on that page. The pictures will also help you to guess the meaning in context. There is a summary of useful vocabulary on the **Check it out** page. Finally, you can use the *Macmillan Essential Dictionary* to consolidate the new vocabulary.

**WEBSITES** There is a list of useful website addresses on page 2. Remember that websites change. Be selective!

## Describing festivals

| | | |
|---|---|---|
| beautiful | colourful | exciting |
| fantastic | happy | local |
| national | noisy | political |
| religious | sad | traditional |

## Some famous festivals

| January | New Year's Day |
|---|---|
| | Chinese New Year* |
| February | Carnival* |
| | Mardi Gras* |
| | Pancake Day* |
| | Eid* |
| | Lent* |
| | Valentine's Day (Europe and North America) |
| March/April | Easter* |
| | Muslim New Year* |
| | Indian New Year* |
| | Hanshik (Korea)* |
| May | May Day |
| June | Valentine's Day (Brazil) |
| July | Independence Day (U.S.A.) |
| | Bastille Day (France) |
| August | O-bon* (Japan) |
| September | Jewish New Year* |
| October | Columbus Day |
| | Halloween |
| | Ramadan* |
| | Diwali* |
| November | All Souls Day |
| | All Saints Day |
| | Day of the Dead |
| | Bonfire Night |
| | Thanksgiving |
| December | Hannukah* |
| | Christmas Eve |
| | Christmas Day |
| | New Year's Eve |
| | Hogmanay |

**Note:** The exact dates of the festivals marked with * change from year to year.

## Verbs for festivals

| | | |
|---|---|---|
| celebrate | commemorate | decorate |
| dress up | enjoy | remember |
| wear | welcome | |

## Nouns

| | | |
|---|---|---|
| ancestor | anniversary | band |
| bonfire | calendar | candle |
| costume | custom | death |
| decoration | disguise | fancy-dress |
| fireworks | float | grave |
| lantern | mask | music |
| musician | procession | spectators |
| symbol | | |

## Internet Websites

We used several Internet websites to research 'Festivals'. Some of these contain extra material that you may find useful. All of them were 'live' at the date of publication. Add your own favourite sites to this list.

Chinese New Year: **www.chinapage.com/newyear.html**
Pancake Day in the UK: **www.bbc.co.uk/religion**
Quebec City Snow Carnival: **www.carnaval.qc.ca**
London Carnival: **www.nottinghillcarnival.org.uk**
Thanksgiving (USA): **www.wilstar.com/holidays/thanksgv.htm**
Mexican Day of the Dead: **www.mexconnect.com/mex_/
 dayofdead.html**

## Let's begin with the New Year...

Make a note of the New Year celebrations in your community. Are there different ways to celebrate?

FESTIVAL EYE

## Which New Year?

Every year has a first day:
New Year's Day. Do you know
when this is? Easy, isn't it?
1st January!

Well - yes and no! Some New Years
are on different dates. This depends on
the calendar. Let's look at some facts.

## Dates

In the Western World, the New Year usually
begins on 1st January. But there are exceptions.
The Muslim New Year begins in March or April. So
does the Indian New Year. But the Jewish New Year
begins in September.

Then there's the Chinese New Year. This begins in January
or February. The Chinese have a lunar calendar,
so the beginning and end of every month depends on the
moon. There are 12 months in their year, and every year has
a different sign – and personality. There are 12 signs, so a sign
comes back every 12 years. The Chinese calendar is very old:
the western year 2005 is the Chinese year 4702 (the year of
the Rooster). And so 2006 is the Chinese year 4703 (the year
of the Dog). The Chinese New Year is a big holiday in many
parts of Asia.

## Celebrating

There's one important thing about New Year in every culture:
it's a time to celebrate! We 'kill' the old year, and all its
problems, and we welcome the New Year. It's a new beginning,
a time of optimism.

Sometimes the New Year celebrations represent different
traditions. For example, in Rio de Janeiro on 31st December,
there are fireworks and concerts on the beach. And there is
also the *Iemanjá* festival with fires and candles and little
boats. Two different ways of saying 'goodbye' to the old year
and of welcoming the future.

### WORD FILE

| | |
|---|---|
| calendar | The organisation of the months in the year. |
| celebrate (v) | To remember an event. |
| celebration | The memory of an event. |
| lunar | Connected with the moon. |
| optimism | A positive feeling. |
| sign | A symbol. |
| tradition | An old way of doing things. |
| welcome (v) | To greet a new person or event. |

🇺🇸 colorful    🇬🇧 colourful

# Chinese New Year

Chinese people clean their houses on the last day of the old year. On New Year's Day, they put on new clothes, and visit their families and friends. Young people receive red envelopes from their parents – with money inside.

Fantastic fireworks are part of the New Year celebrations. There are processions in the streets, and people carry the animal symbol of the new year.

There is special food, too. It's bad luck to kill an animal at New Year, so this food is often vegetarian.

The Chinese New Year Festival is really important: it continues for 15 days. Shops and offices only close for 5 days, but it's a big holiday in many parts of Asia.

On the last day, there's a Festival of Lanterns. People carry lights in the street. It's beautiful.

FESTIVAL EYE

Is there any special food for New Year in your culture? How can you describe it?

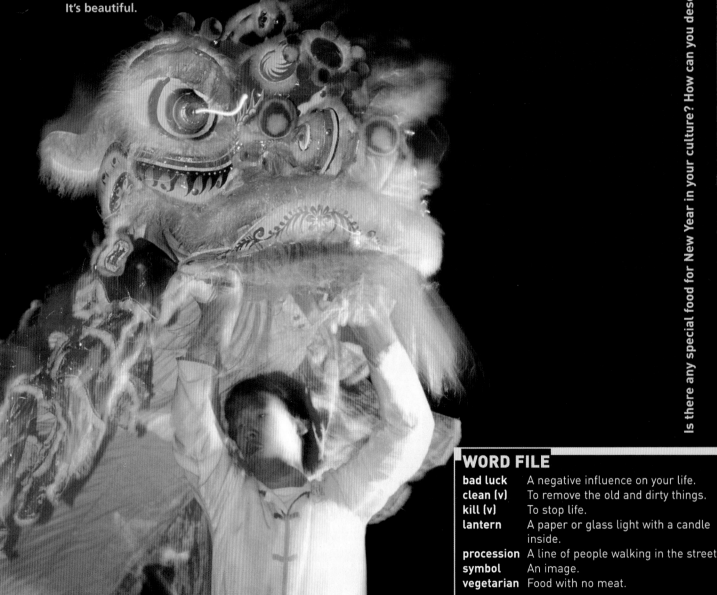

## WORD FILE

| | |
|---|---|
| **bad luck** | A negative influence on your life. |
| **clean (v)** | To remove the old and dirty things. |
| **kill (v)** | To stop life. |
| **lantern** | A paper or glass light with a candle inside. |
| **procession** | A line of people walking in the street |
| **symbol** | An image. |
| **vegetarian** | Food with no meat. |

# Scottish New Year

In this northern part of Britain, the name for New Year's Eve is Hogmanay. The winter nights are cold and long: it gets dark before 4 o'clock, and the sun doesn't rise until nearly 9. It's good to have a festival at this time.

The first stranger to enter the house in the new year brings luck if he carries a piece of coal. The coal is a symbol of warmth for the next year. Sometimes it can be a piece of biscuit (to represent food), or a bottle of whisky (to symbolise happiness). And a tall, dark stranger brings a lot of luck!

There is music and dancing around midnight – and in some places, a big bonfire. People throw old things into the fire. They represent the old year.

The biggest Hogmanay Party is in Edinburgh. It lasts for four days and people come from all over the world. They listen to the bands, dance and sing, watch the fireworks and have a good time.

## BAD WEATHER!

On 31st December 2003, the afternoon was cold. It was winter. Then, suddenly, two hours before midnight, it began to snow. The wind got stronger and stronger. The tents for the musicians collapsed. The wind was too strong for fireworks. It was very dangerous. So the City authorities had to tell 100,000 people: "Sorry. No party tonight! But come back next year…".

### WORD FILE

| | |
|---|---|
| **bonfire** | A fire people build outside at parties or celebrations. |
| **coal** | A black substance that makes a good fire. |
| **collapse (v)** | To fall down. |
| **happiness** | The noun from 'happy'. |
| **rise (v)** | To go up. |
| **snow (v)** | When snow begins to fall. |
| **stranger** | An unknown person. |
| **throw (v)** | To send an object through the air with your hand. |
| **tradition** | An old way of doing things. |
| **warmth** | The noun from 'warm'. |

 cookie     biscuit
symbolize          symbolise

 FESTIVAL EYE

**How did you celebrate New Year? What about your friends?**

5

# Festival Food

## RECIPE

**Make your own pancakes!**

**Ingredients**

250 g flour
3 eggs
2 large spoons sugar
600 ml milk
salt
butter for frying

**Method**

Put the flour, salt and sugar in a big bowl. In another bowl, whisk the eggs and the milk. Add this slowly to the flour mixture. Beat it very well with a wooden spoon. Leave to stand for an hour.

Melt a piece of butter into a small, thick frying pan. When the butter begins to go brown, pour in a little of the mixture. Let it make a thin 'coat' in the pan. Then turn it over and cook the other side.

Put the pancake on a plate. Spread a little more butter on it, some sugar, and some lemon juice. Keep the pancake warm. Make more pancakes.

Eat the pancakes *quickly*.

NOTE: The best pancakes are very, very thin!

 Find a recipe for a special festival food. Better idea: prepare and eat it!

## MARCH-APRIL
## Pancake Tuesday (UK/France)

In the Christian calendar, Lent begins on Ash Wednesday. Mardi Gras (Fat Tuesday) is the last day of Carnival.

Why? Well, many people don't eat meat, milk or eggs during Lent. So on the last day before Lent, they have a big meal to eat up all this food. And with the milk, eggs and butter, they make pancakes.

In Britain, the name of this day is Pancake Day. In some places, there are pancake competitions. There is a famous pancake race in Olney, a village in the south of England. People run 400 metres, throwing their pancakes in the air at the same time.

### WORD FILE

| | |
|---|---|
| **beat (v)** | To mix something quickly. |
| **blow up (v)** | To inflate. |
| **commemorate (v)** | To do something to remember a person or event. |
| **eat up (v)** | To eat everything. |
| **effigy** | A model of a person. |
| **melt (v)** | When a solid becomes liquid. |
| **race (v)** | To run in a competition. |
| **share (v)** | To divide something between two or more people. |
| **sticky** | It adheres to your fingers. |
| **thin** | Only a few millimetres high. |
| **traditional** | Done in the same way for many years. |
| **whisk (v)** | To beat eggs and milk quickly, so that air enters. |

| 🇺🇸 | 🇬🇧 |
|---|---|
| favorite | favourite |
| meter | metre |
| millimeter | millimetre |
| molasses | treacle |
| pan | tin |

## NOVEMBER
# Bonfire Night (UK)

This is a great night for bonfires and fireworks in Britain. In 1605, Guy Fawkes wanted to blow up the English Parliament (with the King inside) in London. He chose a day in November, but he didn't succeed. Today, people still commemorate the event on 5th November. Children make an effigy of Guy Fawkes, and collect money.

Then they burn the effigy on a bonfire.

November is a cold time of the year in Britain. So people eat hot sausages, and gingerbread while they watch the fireworks.

# Thanksgiving (US)

This is a very important North American festival. It is a national holiday, and people like to celebrate it with their families.

The Thanksgiving Dinner is a 'thank you' for the good things in the past year.

It is also an opportunity to share these things with your family and friends. It is always on the fourth Thursday of the month.

The Thanksgiving Dinner commemorates the Pilgrim Fathers in North America. In 1621, they had a feast to celebrate their first year in New England. They ate birds and deer and local fruit and vegetables.

Today turkey and cranberries, with pumpkin pie and sweet potatoes, are the favourite food for this festival.

FESTIVAL EYE

## DECEMBER
# Christmas Eve
**(Italy/France/East Europe) Christmas Day (UK)**

In some countries, people go to church at midnight on 24th December (Christmas Eve) and eat a big meal. This is often fish.

On Christmas Day, the traditional food is roast turkey, or goose, or chicken, or ham, or beef. And lots of different vegetables. And Christmas Pudding, and mince pies… A lot of food!

Many people like to eat special cakes at Christmas. In Italy, panettone is popular. This is a light cake of eggs and dried fruit and vanilla. It is traditional to give a panettone to friends when you visit them at Christmas. So some of these cakes 'travel' a lot. It's a problem if they return to the first 'giver'!

*Explain a special festival meal in your culture to a foreign penpal.*

# RECIPE

## Make your own English Gingerbread!

**Ingredients**
225 g flour
225 g black treacle
450 g oatmeal
75 g melted butter
100 g dark brown sugar
2 teaspoons ground ginger

**Method**
Mix all the dry ingredients together. Make a hole in the middle and pour in the treacle and the butter.
Mix it well.
Put the mixture into a buttered cake tin. Cook in the oven at 170 for one and a half hours.

NOTE: Store it in a tin for several days before you eat it. It's really dark and sticky!

# Your Carnival...
# My Carnival...
# Whose
# Carnival?!

CARNIVAL. From "carne vale", which means "meat goodbye". The last days before the 40 days of Lent in the Christian calendar. It is a time for celebration, eating, music and dancing. It began with the Romans and developed with local variations in many parts of the world.

"Everyone knows about Carnival in Brazil. Rio... Salvador... Recife: their Carnivals are famous all over the world. The music, costumes, and dancing attract tourists from different parts of Brazil and from different countries. Brazilian Carnival is special. What about other Carnivals? Are they the same? Are they different? Let's go on a world tour and take a look at a few others."

## THE AMERICAS

### QUEBEC: SNOW CARNIVAL (temperature: −37°C or −36.4°F!)
Carnival in this French-Canadian city offers: races with dog-sledges, an ice palace, competitions to make snow statues, bands, clowns, and lots of snowmen. The carnival mascot is Bonhomme, a special snowman with a red belt and a big smile.

### NEW ORLEANS: CARNIVAL BALLS AND BEADS
This was a French city. Now it's famous for jazz – and Carnival (Mardi Gras). Groups of people have private parties in the days before Mardi Gras. Every school has one. And then, on Mardi Gras, there are processions and bands. People throw bead necklaces from the floats. The crowds try to catch them.

### ARGENTINA: CARNIVAL DANCES
In the north of Argentina, in the Andes, there are processions and music in the streets. People dance the zamba. (This isn't the same as the Brazilian samba! It is a very slow, traditional Argentinian dance.) They also sing special songs and play harps and accordions.

## EUROPE

### NICE: FLOWERS AND GROTESQUES
This part of France is famous for its flowers. Thousands and thousands of wonderful flower heads and petals decorate the floats. There are battles with flowers. The air is full of the perfum of flowers.
And then there are the 'grotesques': big pasteboard characters. Dragons and demons, witches and giants. Famous artists design these big creatures.
Nice attracts musicians and dancers from other countries: samba from Brazil, soca from Trinidad, musicians from Germany and the West Indies. It's international, but it's also special to Nice... and unique.

### VENICE: ROMANTIC CARNIVAL
The Venice Carnival was famous in the 18th century. This beautiful city is an ideal 'theatre' for fantastic costumes and masks. In winter, there is often fog. It rises from the canals and it hides the buildings. The narrow streets and little squares are very mysterious.
Today, people come to Venice to be part of the city's magic atmosphere. They pretend to be characters from the 18th century, or fantastic imaginary creatures.
Children and adults dress as clowns, as Harlequin, as film characters. There is music, and fireworks... and you can smell doughnuts in the air. People wear masks, so nobody can recogn them. Some of the masks are traditional, and some of them are fantastic.
It's a magic carnival!

How many different Carnivals do you know? What can you discover about them?

• FESTIVAL EYE •

## WORD FILE

| | |
|---|---|
| **accordion** | A musical instrument: you push and pull the two sides to make music. |
| **attract (v)** | To make people want to come. |
| **ball** | A big party, with dancing. |
| **band** | A group of musicians. |
| **battle** | A big fight with a lot of people. |
| **bead** | A small, round part of a necklace. Often of glass or plastic. |
| **doughnuts** | Fried cakes, covered with sugar. |
| **fantastic** | Amazing. |
| **float** | A decorated moving platform with singers, dancers and musicians. |
| **fog** | Grey vapour like clouds. |
| **harp** | A musical instrument with a lot of strings. |
| **mysterious** | Very strange and full of mystery. |
| **pasteboard** | Several layers of paper make a light, strong material. |
| **procession** | A line of people walking in the street. |
| **recognise (v)** | To know someone from their appearance. |
| **snowman** | An effigy made of snow. |
| **theatre** | A place for actors. |
| **traditional** | Done in an old way. |

| 🇺🇸 | 🇬🇧 |
|---|---|
| donut | doughnut |
| movie | film |
| recognize | recognise |
| theater | theatre |
| sled | sledge |
| vapor | vapour |

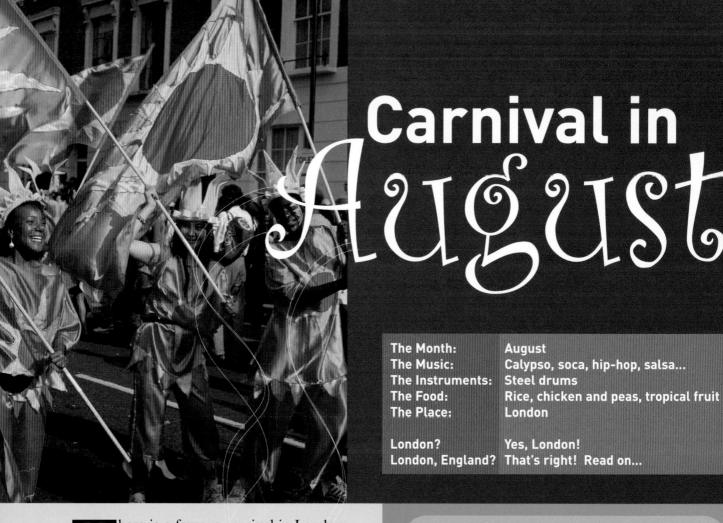

# Carnival in August

| | |
|---|---|
| **The Month:** | August |
| **The Music:** | Calypso, soca, hip-hop, salsa... |
| **The Instruments:** | Steel drums |
| **The Food:** | Rice, chicken and peas, tropical fruit |
| **The Place:** | London |
| | |
| **London?** | Yes, London! |
| **London, England?** | That's right!  Read on... |

There is a famous carnival in London: **Notting Hill Carnival.** It's different from many carnivals. For one thing, it happens in August, not February or March. And London is in Europe, but the Notting Hill Carnival is West Indian! Why? Well, Trinidad is an island in the West Indies. And back in 1833, the slaves in Trinidad became free. And every year they remember this at Carnival time. They celebrate with calypso music and dance.

What's the link between Trinidad and London? See the History Note on the right.

Now more than two million people take part in this special carnival in the Notting Hill area of London. (Remember the 'Notting Hill' movie, with Julia Roberts and Hugh Grant?) There are steel bands, floats, processions, music, and West Indian food. Black and white people dance to calypso and soca in the streets of London!

## WORD FILE

| | |
|---|---|
| **emigrate (v)** | To go and live in a different country. |
| **slaves** | People who are not free. |
| **West Indies** | The islands in the Caribbean. |

 gasoline container    petrol container

## HISTORY NOTE
**QUESTION:** What's the connection with London?
**ANSWER:** A bit of history! You see, Trinidad was part of the British Empire until 1962.

It became independent on 31st August, 1962. And a lot of people from Trinidad (and the other islands in the West Indies) emigrated to Britain in the 1950s. They wanted to have a carnival there – but the weather in London in February is very cold!

So… they chose the last weekend and Monday in August. It's a public holiday in Britain. And the weather's usually warm.

## MUSIC NOTE
**Notting Hill Carnival Glossary**
**Mas:** The costumed processions and floats.
**Calypso:** Traditional Trinidadian music.
**Soca:** The modern, more energetic form of calypso.
**Steelpan:** Traditional Trinidadian instrument. It's made from empty petrol containers.

 **FESTIVAL EYE** What musical instruments are part of Carnival Find pictures and information about them.

# Life and Death

Some festivals celebrate life, and others celebrate death. In many cultures, there are special festivals to remember our ancestors. Here are a few examples. The cultures and countries are very different, but the festivals are very similar.

## KOREA: HANSHIK

This festival is in April. People visit the graves of their ancestors. They remember the dead members of their family.

## JAPAN: O-BON

In the middle of August, there is an important festival to remember their ancestors. People travel home to be with their families. They believe that their dead relatives return. They put lanterns in their houses, to guide them. They also provide food for their ancestors: fruit and vegetables.

## HALLOWEEN AND THE DAY OF THE DEAD

| 31st October | Halloween |
| --- | --- |
| 1st November | All Saints Day |
| 2nd November | All Souls Day |
| | (The Day of the Dead) |

Halloween was a pre-Christian festival to celebrate the dead. Then it became part of the Christian festivals to remember dead people. Some people used to think that the dead come out of their graves at Halloween. In some countries, people dress up as witches or ghosts. This festival is now very popular in the United States.

In Mexico, the Day of the Dead is a very famous celebration. People travel to their family homes and visit the graves of their dead ancestors. There are sweets in the shape of skulls, and special cakes. There are skeletons and skulls as decorations. They decorate the graves with orange flowers. The festival is about death, but it isn't sad.

**Halloween is famous in lots of countries. What do you know about it? Compare information with a friend and make a poster about this festival.**

## WORD FILE

| | |
| --- | --- |
| **ancestor** | The people in your family before you. |
| **ghost** | A spirit. |
| **grave** | The place in the earth where dead people are buried. |
| **relative** | A member of your family. |
| **skeleton** | All the bones of a person. |
| **skull** | The bones in a person's head. |
| **witch** | A magical female person. |

🇺🇸 candy    🇬🇧 sweets

FESTIVAL EYE

# *Family* Festivals

NEW YEAR AND CARNIVAL ARE BIG, PUBLIC FESTIVALS. BUT THERE ARE LOTS OF SMALLER, 'PRIVATE' ONES, TOO. SOME FESTIVALS ARE NATIONAL, OR BELONG TO SPECIAL GROUPS OF PEOPLE. SOME OF THEM CELEBRATE A NATIONAL EVENT, LIKE INDEPENDENCE.

▶ LET'S TAKE A LOOK AT SOME OF THESE. WHICH ONES DO YOU RECOGNISE?

- ◯ Teacher's Day
- ◯ Children's Day
- ◯ Women's Day
- ◯ World Environment Day
- ◯ Mother's Day
- ◯ Father's Day
- ◯ Birthday
- ◯ Name Day
- ◯ Valentine's Day
- ◯ Columbus Day

▶▶ HERE ARE SOME DESCRIPTIONS OF THESE EVENTS. WHICH DESCRIPTION GOES WITH WHICH FESTIVAL?

1. A very personal festival: it commemorates your first day here!
2. Children give presents to their mums to say 'thank you'.
3. Another personal festival. In some cultures, it commemorates a saint.
4. Children are the focus of this October festival.
5. 15th October is a good day for teachers!
6. The festival for lovers. It is a saint's day on 14th. February in some countries.
7. Dad deserves a big hug!
8. Christopher Columbus wanted to go to Asia, but he sailed to the New World.
9. An international green festival on 5th June.
10. Women support women on this day in March.

(Answers on page 16.)

**WORD FILE**

| | |
|---|---|
| **personal** | Belongs to a person. |
| **private** | Not public. |
| **public** | Belongs to everyone. |

🇺🇸 mom    🇬🇧 mum
recognize    recognise

FESTIVAL EYE

Choose three of these festivals, or three similar ones in your region. What happens at them? Why are they important?

# raps, songs and rhymes

*from*

*to*

## Valentine's Day
Roses are red,
Lavender's blue,
Sugar is sweet
And so are you!
Be my Valentine.

## Bonfire Night
Please remember
The fifth of November,
Gunpowder, treason and plot.
I see no reason
Why gunpowder, treason
Should ever be forgot!
Penny for the Guy! Penny for the Guy!

## Christmas
Jingle bells, Jingle bells,
Jingle all the way,
Oh what fun it is to go
In a one-horse open sleigh!

## Christmas/New Year
We wish you a Merry Christmas,
We wish you a Merry Christmas,
We wish you a Merry Christmas
And a Happy New Year!

## Hogmanay (the language is Scottish!)
Should auld acquaintance be forgot,
And never brought to mind,
Should auld acquaintance be forgot,
For the sake of auld lang syne.

## Birthdays
Happy birthday to you,
Happy birthday to you,
Happy birthday, dear ...  (name),
Happy birthday to you!

### WORD FILE

| | |
|---|---|
| **acquaintance** | A person you know. |
| **auld lang syne** | Things in the past (Scottish). |
| **forgot** | Forgotten (Scottish). |
| **for the sake of** | Because of. |
| **gunpowder** | An explosive powder. |
| **one-horse** | Pulled by one horse. |
| **plot** | A conspiracy. |
| **sleigh** | A sled/sledge. |
| **treason** | An action against your country. |

🇺🇸 sled  🇬🇧 sledge

**FESTIVAL EYE**

**Collect some more Festival songs
or rhymes from your country.**

# Do you know?

(Answers on page 16.)

## 1. CARNIVAL QUIZ

**A** Who had the first Carnival?
i The Romans    ii The Greeks    iii The Egyptians

**B** What did people say 'goodbye' to at Carnival?
i fruit    ii vegetables    iii meat

**C** What is the meaning of the French adjective for the last day of Carnival?
i big    ii happy    iii fat

**D** Lent comes after Carnival. How many days is it?
i 30    ii 40    iii 50

**E** When is Carnival in London?
i February    ii August    iii December

## 2. PLANTS AND FESTIVALS

**A** Which country has a cherry blossom festival?
i Japan    ii China    iii India

**B** Where did the first Christmas trees come from?
i England    ii Germany    iii Australia

**C** Which colour rose means 'I love you'?
i red rose    ii yellow rose    iii pink rose

**D** What colour flowers do Mexicans use on the Day of the Dead?
i red    ii yellow    iii orange

**E** What vegetable do people use at Halloween?
i potato    ii pumpkin    iii onion

## 3. RELIGIONS AND FESTIVALS

**A** Eid is a festival for
i Muslims    ii Protestants    iii Catholics

**B** The Indian community celebrates Diwali with
i light    ii fire    iii flowers

**C** At the Chinese New Year, it is bad luck to
i kill an animal    ii cook food    iii eat fruit

**D** On the Mexican Day of the Dead, people eat sugar
i skulls    ii skeletons    iii flowers

**E** Whose birthday do people celebrate in many Asian countries?
i their ancestors    ii Buddha    iii the symbol of the new year

## 4. WORD BOX

**Find 13 festivals or parts of festivals.**
**Use the word box to answer the clues.**

```
T X C F D E A D R S L V A Q I
E C D O S A F Z B O E S K H X
T H A N K S G I V I N G W A E
X R G E S T X R T D T O A L Y
E I D A U E K J H F D O X L J
N S V H F R A M A D A N H O X
X T K L H I U F N M X D U W V
Y M S Q A Y B K L T B F O E I
V A L E N T I N E B M T S E Y
B S R G S U K L M H A I X N L
M E V Y H M A R D I G R A S T
C A R N I V A L W X D R F S X
H T M S K E V X T D I W A L I
```

### Across

1. A very famous festival in Mexico.
2. North Americans remember the past.
3. A big Muslim festival.
4. Another important Muslim festival.
5. One festival; two dates.
6. Brazil is famous for it.
7. Indians celebrate it with lights.
8. French Tuesday. / The fat part of Tuesday.

### Down

9. Many people hope that this will be white.
10. In Korea, they remember their ancestors.
11. Lots of eggs to eat.
12. Look out for witches!
13. The period of 40 days before Easter.

 color     colour

# Projects

## Cultural Research

Choose a different culture. Find out about one of its festivals. Present your information on a poster.

## 1 New Year

Find a community which celebrates New Year in a different way from you. Research the traditions. Present your information about it.

## 2 Festival Calendar

Look at the list of festivals on page 2. Which ones do you celebrate in your culture? There are lots of other festivals, too. Make a personal Festival Year Calendar. You can organise it like this:

|  | INTERNATIONAL | RELIGIOUS | NATIONAL |
|---|---|---|---|
| January |  | ●●●●● |  |
| February |  |  | ●●●●● |
| March |  |  |  |
| April |  | ●●●●● |  |
| May |  |  | ●●●●● |
| June |  |  | ●●●●● |
| July | ●●●●● |  |  |
| etc. |  |  |  |

## 3 Masks

Look at the pictures of Carnival on pages 8 and 9. Choose a character and design your own mask. It can be beautiful, fantastic or scary. Have an exhibition. If possible, make and wear your mask. How do you feel in it?

## 5 Carnival and Samba

What can you discover about Samba Schools in Brazil? Make an album to inform your friends.

## 6 Festival Detective

What is your favourite festival? How much can you find out about it? When did it begin? Why? Where? Design a tourist booklet to explain it to foreign visitors.

Collect all your Festival Eye work. Make a poster to show the things that you discovered.

## 7 Easter Eggs

In Eastern Europe, people decorate eggs for Easter. How about you? Boil an egg until it is hard. Then paint a design on it. Have an Easter Egg display. You can have prizes for the most beautiful egg, the funniest egg, the most colourful egg.

| colorful | colourful |
|---|---|
| favorite | favourite |
| organize | organise |

# Topics chatrooms

## Teens chat

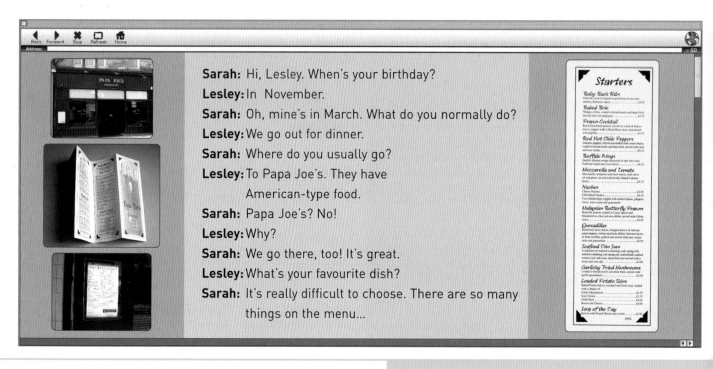

**Sarah:** Hi, Lesley. When's your birthday?
**Lesley:** In November.
**Sarah:** Oh, mine's in March. What do you normally do?
**Lesley:** We go out for dinner.
**Sarah:** Where do you usually go?
**Lesley:** To Papa Joe's. They have American-type food.
**Sarah:** Papa Joe's? No!
**Lesley:** Why?
**Sarah:** We go there, too! It's great.
**Lesley:** What's your favourite dish?
**Sarah:** It's really difficult to choose. There are so many things on the menu...

## Can you believe it?

On 14th February, lots of people in Britain put Valentine's Day messages in the newspapers. Here are a few of them.

**Jill:** Be my Valentine this year, next year, forever! Much love, Jack.

Cinderella, I have a beautiful glass slipper for you. Call after 8 p.m. Prince.

1000 red roses for my love. Romeo.

Valentine greetings to Napoleon from your fan-club.

## Facts Check

**Page 12**  1. Birthday; 2. Mother's Day;
3. Name Day; 4. Children's Day;
5. Teacher's Day; 6. Valentine's Day;
7. Father's Day; 8. Columbus Day;
9. World Environment Day;
10. Women's Day

**Page 14**  1. **CARNIVAL QUIZ:** A-i; B-iii; C-iii; D-ii; E-ii

2. **PLANTS AND FESTIVALS:** A-i; B-ii; C-i; D-iii; E-ii

3. **RELIGIONS AND FESTIVALS:** A-i; B-i; C-i; D-i; E-ii

4. **WORD BOX: Across:** 1. DEAD;
2. THANKSGIVING; 3. EID; 4. RAMADAN;
5. VALENTINE; 6. CARNIVAL; 7. DIWALI;
8. MARDI GRAS;
**Down:** 9. CHRISTMAS; 10. HANSHIK;
11. EASTER; 12. HALLOWEEN; 13. LENT

*Bye for now!*
*That's the end of 'Festivals'. Of course, you can continue with your Festival Eye work. See you in the next Topics title. Bye!*

Susan Holden